Top
Most Delicious
Puff Pastry Recipes

All rights reserved.
Otherworld Publishing
Copyright © 2016

Disclaimer

Otherworld Publishing and its authors have used their best efforts in preparing these pages and their publications. Otherworld Publishing and its authors make no warranty of any kind, expressed or implied, with regard to the information supplied.

Limits of Liability

Otherworld Publishing and its authors shall not be liable in the event of incidental or consequential damages or injury in connection with, or arising out of, the providing of the information offered here.

Introduction

Puff pastry is the definition of elegant simplicity. With decadent buttery layers of light, flaky dough, along with incredible versatility, puff pastry is an essential component of effortless yet sophisticated baking.

Puff pastry is a classic staple that can serve as a base to many types of dishes. As you will find in this recipe book, puff pastry can be used to create a delicious breakfast, tasty snacks, amazing desserts and even dinner dishes.

The secret to cooking with puff pastry is that once you have the dough, the remainder of a recipe is quite simple. While a recipe for homemade puff pastry is included at the beginning of this book, each recipe listed would be just as delicious if made with store purchased pastry dough. The choice between using store bought or handmade dough is your own, however the key is to plan ahead or keep some consistently stocked in your freezer. The recipes in this recipe book require a relatively short amount of time to prep and cook. However, if you have no dough on hand and plan to make it yourself, plan on a bit of time and effort being expended. Making pastry dough is a time consuming practice, plus there is additional time required to freeze the dough prior to use.

When frozen, puff pastry is similar to pie dough. It looks thick and a bit heavy. Yet when puff pastry bakes it puffs up, oftentimes the baked dough will be several times its pre-baked thickness. Baking the dough forces a reaction between the fat (the butter) and the air in the dough, resulting in layer upon layer of thin, flaky sheets. This is why prior to using the dough needs to be kept in the freezer.

Puff pastry dishes may lose some of their flakiness and become a bit soft if left out for too long. Therefore, these recipes will be most delicious if they are served shortly after having been removed from the oven.

Contents

Dough *1*

   0. Basic Puff Pastry Dough 2

Savory *3*

   1. Tomato and Cheese Tart 4
   2. Chicken and Pesto Pizza 5
   3. Beet and Turnip Galette 6
   4. Asparagus Pie 8
   5. Ricotta, Salami, Asparagus Tart 9
   6. French Onion Puffs 11
   7. Brie and Jam Pastry Bites 13
   8. Baked Egg Cups 14
   9. Cheese Straws 15
  10. Breakfast Hand Pies 16
  11. Bean and Chicken Empanadas 17
  12. Spinach and Feta Turnovers 19
  13. Mini Herb Cups 20
  14. Kale and Olive Hand Pies 21
  15. Rosemary Artichoke Tart 23
  16. Sausage Roll 25
  17. Zucchini Ricotta Tart 26
  18. Pesto Tart 28
  19. Prosciutto and Pesto Puffs 30
  20. Smoked Salmon Puffs 31
  21. Pastry Sliders 32
  22. Shrimp Wrapped Puff 33

23. Curry and Beef Pie 34
24. Puff Pastry "Caps" 36

Sweet 37

25. Apple Tart 38
26. Glazed Raspberry Strudel 39
27. Apple Apricot Tart 41
28. Strawberry Napoleons 42
29. Apple Strudel 44
30. Rhubarb Galette 46
31. Strawberry Balsamic Tartlets 48
32. Nutella Pastry Puffs 50
33. Cinnamon Twists 51
34. Nutella Roll Ups 53
35. Peach and Goat Cheese Turn Overs 54
36. Triple Berry Tart 56
37. Puff Candy Bites 57
38. Nutella Pastry 58
39. Coconut Pumpkin Roll Ups 59
40. Raspberry Lemon Napoleons 60
41. Cinnamon Puffs 61
42. Pear Ginger Tart 62
43. Peach Tart 63
44. Berry Cheesecake 64
45. Apple Caramel Tartlets 66
46. Raspberry and Brie Hand Pies 67
47. Meyer Lemon Tart 69
48. Bite Sized Strawberry Pastries 71
49. White Chocolate Raspberry Tart 72
50. Chocolate Banoffee Pie 73

Top 50 Most Delicious Puff Pastry Recipes

Dough

Basic Puff Pastry Dough

Give yourself plenty of time when making this dough, as it requires a great deal of patience. Rest assured that the end product would be well worth the effort, as this recipe will produce flaky, buttery, delicious puff pastry.

Yield: 1 ½ pounds of dough

Ingredients:
2 cups all-purpose flour
2 ½ sticks butter, unsalted and cold
½ cups cold water
1 teaspoon salt

Method of Preparation:
1. Slice two sticks of the butter into half an inch thick cubes, and return to the fridge.
2. Combine water and salt, mix to dissolve and set aside.
3. Take remaining ½ stick of butter and chop coarsely.
4. Sift flour into food processor, and blend with the ½ stick of butter just chopped until absorbed.
5. Retrieve remaining butter from fridge and combine in food processor, pulse twice to mix.
6. Add salt water and pulse until dough forms, taking care not to over mix.
7. Lightly flour counter, and scrape dough onto surface.
8. Make a rectangle shape out of the dough, and place in between two sheets of plastic wrapping.
9. Use a rolling pin to flatten dough, ultimately shaping out a 12 x 18 inch sheet.
10. Freeze until firm, at least one hour.

Top 50 Most Delicious Puff Pastry Recipes

SAVORY

Tomato and Cheese Tart

This tart is a simple recipe that yields an incredibly delicious meal. It is substantial enough to stand on its own as a simple lunch, or served with a salad would make a fine dinner. Savory and nutritious, this tart is a guaranteed success.

Yield: 1 Tart

Ingredients:
1 sheet frozen puff pastry
2 tablespoons basil, fresh and chopped
½ cup cheddar cheese, shredded
½ cup mozzarella cheese, shredded
3 tablespoons mayonnaise
2 tomatoes, sliced thin
Salt and Pepper to taste

Method of Preparation:
1. Preheat oven to 400 degrees.
2. After slicing tomatoes, place between sheets of paper towel and let dry for a minimum of thirty minutes.
3. During this time, retrieve the pastry sheet from the freezer and let sit at room temperature.
4. Line a baking sheet with parchment paper, and unfold pastry onto sheet.
5. To avoid dough puffing up during baking, insert a fork throughout the dough as well as around the edges.
6. Pinch or fold up the edges of the dough to form a crust.
7. Spoon the mayonnaise on the pastry surface into a thin layer.
8. Evenly distribute shredded cheese and then tomatoes.
9. Salt and pepper generously, then top with chopped basil.
10. Bake for 30 minutes or until the cheese has melted and the edges are golden.
11. Allow to cool for five minutes before serving.

Chicken and Pesto Pizza

Chicken and pesto combine with rich melted cheese for a healthy and delicious, grease-free pizza alternative. A more elegant approach to the take out standby, this is a far superior variation that will quickly become a favorite recipe.

Yield: 1 Pizza

Ingredients:
1 Sheet frozen puff pastry
½ cup mozzarella cheese, shredded
2 tablespoons Parmesan, grated
3 tablespoons pesto
1 tablespoon olive oil
1 cup chicken breast, cooked and diced
Salt and Pepper

Method of Preparation:
1. Preheat oven to 400 degrees.
2. Retrieve puff pastry sheet from freezer and let sit at room temperature for 30 minutes prior to using.
3. Line a baking sheet with parchment paper, and unfold pastry onto sheet.
4. To avoid dough puffing up during baking, insert a fork throughout the dough as well as around the edges.
5. Pinch or fold up the edges of the dough to form a crust.
6. In a thin layer, cover the pastry with pesto.
7. Arrange diced chicken on tart, and brush with olive oil.
8. Evenly distribute shredded cheese over chicken and dough.
9. Add salt and pepper to taste.
10. Bake for 15 minutes or until the cheese has melted and the edges are golden.
11. Allow to cool for five minutes before serving.

Beet and Turnip Galette

Root vegetables are often overlooked in the kitchen but shine in this simple and delicious recipe. During baking the rich colors deepen, and the result is an incredibly sophisticated looking galette that is sure to surprise you with its depth of flavor.

Yield: 1 Tart

Ingredients:
1 sheet frozen puff pastry
1/2 cup ricotta cheese
1/4 teaspoon smoked paprika
2 tablespoons olive oil
6 turnips
3 beets
Salt to taste

Method of Preparation:
1. Preheat oven to 400 degrees.
2. Remove pastry from freezer and allow to sit at room temperature for at least 30 minutes.
3. Brush turnips and beets with half of the olive oil and sprinkle with salt. Roast for 30 minutes. When you can easily insert a fork, remove them from the oven.
4. Line a baking sheet with parchment paper and unfold pastry dough on top, rounding dough into a circular shape.
5. To avoid dough puffing up during baking, insert a fork throughout the dough as well as around the edges.
6. Evenly spread dough with ricotta cheese, avoiding the outermost edge of the dough by one inch.
7. Pinch or fold up the edges of the dough to create a raised crust, slightly layered over the zucchini and squash.

8. Slice turnips and beets thinly, and layer them over the cheese and pastry.
9. Sprinkle the smoked paprika and remaining olive oil over the pastry.
10. Bake for 20 minutes or until crust is golden.
11. Allow to cool for five minutes before serving.

ASPARAGUS PIE

Make this fresh tasting tart in spring when asparagus is aplenty and at the prime of its harvest. When combined with the cheese the flavors are rich and yet light, resulting in a satisfying but light dish. Serve for a simple lunch for four or as main dish with sides.

Yield: 1 Pie

Ingredients:
1 sheet frozen puff pastry
1 tablespoon olive oil
1 ½ pounds asparagus
2 cups Gruyere cheese
Salt and Pepper

Method of Preparation:
1. Preheat oven to 400 degrees.
2. Remove pastry from freezer and allow to sit at room temperature for at least 30 minutes.
3. Line a baking sheet with parchment paper, and unfold pastry onto sheet.
4. To avoid dough puffing up during baking, insert a fork throughout the dough as well as around the edges.
5. Pinch or fold up the edges of the dough to form a crust.
6. Bake the thawed pastry sheet for fifteen minutes or until crust is lightly browned.
7. Remove from oven and cover with cheese.
8. Arrange asparagus spears over the cheese.
9. Brush with oil and salt and pepper to taste.
10. Bake for another 20 minutes or until you can easily pierce asparagus with a fork.
11. Allow to cool five minutes before slicing into squares.

Ricotta, Salami, Asparagus Tart

Smoky salami and creamy ricotta combine with the fresh taste of asparagus in this unexpected dish. Serve this tart warm when the cheese is still melted for a satisfying, savory, early spring lunch.

Yield: 1 Tart

Ingredients:
1 sheet frozen puff pastry
1 tablespoon olive oil
1 pound asparagus
⅔ cup Gruyere cheese
½ cup ricotta cheese
1 ½ ounces salami, sliced thin
1 egg
Salt and Pepper

Method of Preparation:
1. Preheat oven to 400 degrees.
2. Remove pastry from freezer and allow to sit at room temperature for at least 30 minutes.
3. Line a baking sheet with parchment paper, and unfold pastry onto sheet.
4. To avoid dough puffing up during baking, insert a fork throughout the dough as well as around the edges.
5. Pinch or fold up the edges of the dough to form a crust.
6. In a steamer, cook asparagus spears until slightly tender.
7. Remove from steamer and place in ice water. Allow to cool.
8. Chop top third of asparagus spears off and set aside.
9. In a food processor, blend remaining ⅔ of asparagus until pureed.
10. Crack the egg into a separate bowl and beat until smooth.

11. Combine egg, ricotta cheese, oil and set to puree and mix until combined.
12. Gently fold in salami slices and half of the shredded cheese.
13. Pour mix over pastry and spread evenly.
14. Sprinkle with remaining cheese and asparagus tops.
15. Finally, brush one tablespoon oil over surface of the entire pastry.
16. Bake for 20 minutes or until crust is golden.

FRENCH ONION PUFFS

This recipes takes a perennial favorite, French onion soup, and stuffs it inside a flaky, delicious puff pastry for a new take on a classic. Incredibly sophisticated, serve this dish as a party appetizer to impress your guests.

Yield: 12 Puffs

Ingredients:
2 sheets frozen puff pastry
2 yellow onions, peeled and sliced
2 tablespoons whole grain mustard
1 teaspoon fresh thyme leaves
3 tablespoons unsalted butter
1 tablespoon olive oil
1 teaspoon salt
1/2 teaspoon pepper
1 egg
1/3 cup finely grated Gruyère cheese
Pinch of granulated sugar
3 tablespoons white wine

1. **Method of Preparation:**
2. Preheat oven to 375 degrees.
3. Remove pastry from freezer and allow to sit at room temperature for at least 30 minutes.
4. Over medium heat, melt butter in a medium sauce pan. Add olive oil and stir.
5. Add sliced onions and toss to coat with butter and oil mix.
6. Let onions cook for five minutes then add thyme, pinch of sugar, salt and pepper and stir.
7. Cover pan and continue to cook, stirring occasionally, until onions completely soft and dark.

8. Add white wine, stirring as it caramelizes, for about a minute.
9. Once wine has evaporated, remove from heat and set aside.
10. Line a baking sheet with parchment paper and set aside.
11. Unfold pastry onto lightly floured countertop.
12. Using lightly floured cutter or a glass, press 1 ½ in circles out of pastry squares. There should be 24 pastry circles, at minimum.
13. Place pastry circles on parchment lined baking sheet.
14. In a small bowl, crack and beat egg until smooth, then brush pastry circles with beaten egg.
15. Set aside 12 of the circles, and spread them with a little dollop of mustard. Add a teaspoon of the onions and half a teaspoon of grated cheese.
16. Repeat with all 12 circles.
17. Gently close pastry by pressing the remaining 12 circles on the mix. Be sure to put egged side facing down towards the mix.
18. Carefully close the two circles together using fingers and a fork.
19. Brush finished puffs with remaining egg, and using a toothpick, poke a hole in the top of each puff.
20. Bake for 12 minutes or until golden brown and puffy.
21. Allow to cool for five minutes before serving warm.

Brie and Jam Pastry Bites

Baked brie is a classic favorite that is complemented by the sweet taste of your favorite jam. In this recipe, feel free to use any flavor jam of your liking or whatever you happen to have on hand. These darling bites are individual sized, perfect for pre meal appetizers or a sophisticated snack.

Yield: 24 Bites

Ingredients:
2 sheets frozen puff pastry
1/2 wedge of brie
1/3 cup jam
1 egg
1 tablespoon milk

Method of Preparation:
1. Preheat oven to 375 degrees.
2. Remove pastry from freezer and allow to sit at room temperature for at least 30 minutes.
3. Line a baking sheet with parchment paper and set aside.
4. To make these bites, each sheet of pastry will need to be cut into 24 small rectangles to make 12 rectangle pockets. Once completed, set aside.
5. Crack egg into small bowl and beat until smooth. Combine with tablespoon of milk.
6. Brush the egg wash over 12 of the rectangles.
7. Slice brie into small wedges and set on brushed rectangle.
8. Add half a teaspoon of the jam on top of brie.
9. Layer the second pastry rectangle over the cheese and jam.
10. Using a fork and your fingers, tightly fold the edges together making sure to seal pastry closed.
11. Using a toothpick, poke a small hole into the center of the pastry.
12. Bake for 10 minutes or until crust is golden.

BAKED EGG CUPS

The perfect solution to serving a stress free brunch; the best thing about these egg cups is that you can prep ahead of time. These bake all at once in their own dishes, eliminating concerns about coordinating finishing times. Consider baking in single serving ramekins for a charming and practical individual serving dish.

Yield: 6 Egg Cups

Ingredients:
2 sheets of frozen puff pastry
1 medium potato, cubed
½ yellow onion, diced
2 tablespoons olive oil
2 tablespoons butter, melted
6 eggs
Salt and pepper to taste

Method of Preparation:
1. Remove puff pastry from freezer and allow to sit at room temperature for thirty minutes.
2. Preheat oven to 400 degrees.
3. On a lightly floured surface, slice pastry into squares larger than the dish you will be baking them in.
4. Gently press pastry into each dish.
5. To avoid dough puffing up during baking, insert a fork throughout the dough as well as around the edges, then brush with melted butter.
6. Heat oil in saute pan over medium heat, and add onion and potato, salt and pepper, and cook for several minutes or until just browning.
7. Remove from pan, and evenly distribute over pastry cups.
8. Crack one egg into each cup.
9. Bake for 12 minutes for a medium boiled egg, or adjust time to your liking.

CHEESE STRAWS

This recipe is quick and simple, the perfect solution for an easy snack that anyone is sure to appreciate. Ready in just minutes, it will make enough straws to feed a small group or to seal in an airtight container and nosh on throughout the week.

Yield: 24 Straws

Ingredients:

2 sheets frozen puff pastry
½ cup gruyere cheese, grated
½ cup parmesan cheese, grated
1 teaspoon fresh thyme, minced
1 large egg
Salt and pepper

Method of Preparation:
1. Remove puff pastry from freezer and allow to sit at room temperature for thirty minutes.
2. Line a baking sheet with parchment paper and set aside.
3. Preheat oven to 375 degrees.
4. On a lightly floured surface, roll pastry out flat.
5. In a small bowl, crack egg and add with one tablespoon of water, and beat egg and water until smooth.
6. Brush pastry surface with egg and water mix.
7. Spread half of each type of cheese, half of the thyme, salt and pepper evenly across the dough.
8. Lightly press ingredients into dough with a glass or rolling pin.
9. Cut long, even strips out of dough using a knife or pizza cutter that has been lightly floured.
10. Using your hands, twist each piece and lay on baking sheet.
11. Bake for 10 minutes or until golden.
12. Flip and bake for another minute.
13. Allow to cool before serving.

Breakfast Hand Pies

Savory and flaky, these tarts are incredibly versatile. Make ahead for an ideal breakfast on the go, or bake the morning of and serve with sides for a sophisticated brunch main course.

Yield: 4 Hand Pies

Ingredients:
1 sheet frozen puff pastry
½ cup cheddar cheese, grated
4 eggs
2 tomatoes, sliced
Salt and pepper to taste

Method of Preparation:
1. Preheat oven to 375 degrees.
2. Remove puff pastry from freezer and allow to sit at room temperature for thirty minutes.
3. Line a baking sheet with parchment paper and set aside.
4. On a lightly floured surface, roll pastry out flat.
5. Divide and cut into four equal squares.
6. To avoid dough puffing up during baking, insert a fork throughout the dough as well as around the edges.
7. Pinch or fold up the edges of the dough to form a crust.
8. Bake pastry for 15 minutes or until slightly golden and puffy.
9. Let cool, and then making a well in the center of the pastry, cover with cheese.
10. Crack one egg into each shell, and then add tomato slices.
11. Add salt and pepper to taste.
12. Return to oven and bake until egg is set, about 10 minutes.
13. Serve immediately.

Bean and Chicken Empanadas

A perfect dinner option, these bean and chicken empanadas are stuffed with vegetables and protein for a well-rounded meal. Layers of flaky pastry surround the creamy beans and moist chicken, all seasoned to perfection.

Yield: 8 Empanadas

Ingredients:
4 sheets frozen puff pastry
¼ cup vegetable oil
1 small onion, chopped
2 cloves garlic
1 teaspoon cumin
1 ½ teaspoon oregano
¼ teaspoon cayenne pepper
1 can black beans
1 ½ cup chicken, cooked and shredded
½ cup cilantro, fresh and chopped
Salt and pepper to taste

Method of Preparation:
1. Preheat oven to 375 degrees.
2. Remove puff pastry from freezer and allow to sit at room temperature for thirty minutes.
3. Heat oil in frying pan over medium heat. Sauté garlic and onions until translucent and soft, several minutes. Add spices and stir to combine, then add chicken and black beans. Continue to stir until contents are heated through.
4. Remove from heat and set aside to cool. Sprinkle with cilantro
5. Line a baking sheet with parchment paper and set aside.
6. On a lightly floured surface, roll pastry out flat.

7. Divide and cut each sheet of dough into four equal squares using a lightly floured knife or pizza cutter.
8. To shape and fill empanadas, take one square at a time and turn it so that it is diamond shaped, so that it could be two triangles base to base.
9. Scoop one heaping spoonful of mix onto one triangle of the diamond. Using your fingers or the prongs of a fork, gently fold the other triangle half over the mix, and press along the seam to seal tightly.
10. Repeat with remaining empanadas.
11. Bake for 15 minutes or until golden.
12. Allow to cool for five minutes before serving.

SPINACH AND FETA TURNOVERS

Be transported with this Greek inspired meal. These triangles are simple and savory, filling without being heavy. The layers of flaky pastry combine with the creamy cheese and spinach mix to make an easy and satisfying meal.

Yield: 6 Turn Overs

Ingredients:

2 sheets frozen puff pastry	3 eggs
1 1/2 cups spinach	1 tablespoon water
1 cup feta cheese	1 onion, chopped
3 tablespoons fresh parsley	

Method of Preparation:
1. Remove puff pastry from freezer and allow to sit at room temperature for thirty minutes.
2. Preheat oven to 375 degrees.
3. Line a baking sheet with parchment paper and set aside.
4. On a lightly floured surface, roll pastry out flat.
5. Divide and cut dough into twelve equal squares using a lightly floured knife or pizza cutter.
6. In a medium bowl combine spinach, feta, onion and mix together.
7. Drop one spoonful of filling into six of the squares, avoiding the outermost half of an inch around the edges.
8. Take another square, and enclose filling covered square, firmly sealing edges together with fingers or a fork.
9. Complete with remaining pastries, and transfer to baking sheet.
10. Brush with egg wash.
11. Bake 30 minutes or until golden, allow to cool for five minutes before serving.

MINI HERB CUPS

The ideal party appetizer, serve these individual sized herb cups on your favorite platter or tray for a striking dish that is guaranteed to impress your guests. Ideal to be made ahead of time, you can serve this either warm or at room temperature.

Yield: 36 Mini Cups

Ingredients:
1 sheet frozen puff pastry
1 cup heavy cream
1 cup Swiss cheese, shredded
2 tablespoons shallots, chopped
1 tablespoon basil, fresh and chopped
1 tablespoon chives, chopped
¼ teaspoon black pepper
¼ teaspoon red pepper flakes
3 eggs

Method of Preparation:
1. Preheat oven to 400 degrees.
2. Lightly grease mini muffin tin cups.
3. In a small bowl, beat eggs together until smooth. Combine with cream, shallots, basil, chives, red pepper flakes and black pepper, mix together.
4. Fold cheese into mix.
5. On a lightly floured surface, unroll pastry.
6. Divide and cut dough into 36 equal squares, approximately two inches each.
7. Press each pastry square into a mini muffin tin cup.
8. Scoop one heaping tablespoon of mix into each cup.
9. Bake for 15 minutes or until crust is golden and filling is set.

Kale and Olive Hand Pies

Kale and olives combine for a tart that is filling and nutrient dense. Seasoned with onions and fennel, the taste is rich but not overpowering. The addition of feta cheese adds a final component to this simple to make, yet complex in flavor dish. Consider topping the final product with a dusting of feta just before serving.

Yield: 18 Hand Pies

Ingredients:
2 sheets frozen puff pastry
1/3 cup feta cheese
3 tablespoons unsalted butter, melted
2 tablespoons olive oil
Fresh ground black pepper
1 yellow onion, diced
1 bulb fennel, quartered, cored, and sliced thin
3 cloves garlic, chopped
1 bunch kale, stems removed, chopped into bite-sized pieces
1/4 cup kalamata olives, pitted and chopped
2 tablespoons fresh parsley, chopped

Method of Preparation:
1. Preheat oven to 375 degrees.
2. Remove pastry from freezer and allow to sit at room temperature for at least 30 minutes.
3. Over medium heat, heat oil in a medium frying pan.
4. Add sliced onions and toss to coat.
5. Let onions cook for five minutes until soft and clear, then add garlic and fennel and stir.
6. Cook for an additional five minutes.
7. Add kale, cover, and let simmer until wilted.

8. Remove from heat, and fold in olives, feta and parsley. Add pepper to taste.
9. Line a baking sheet with parchment paper and set aside.
10. Unfold pastry onto lightly floured countertop.
11. Divide and cut dough into 9 equal squares out of each sheet for a total of 18.
12. Pinch or fold up the edges of the dough to create a raised crust, and a well like center for the filling.
13. Scoop a heaping tablespoon of the mix into each tart, and brush with olive oil.
14. Place pastry circles on parchment lined baking sheet.
15. Bake 30 minutes or until golden.

Rosemary Artichoke Tart

Sophisticated flavors, the rosemary and artichoke blend together for a tart that is as easy as it is elegant. Fresh herbs and goat cheese complement the rustic taste of artichokes for a satisfying meal, perfect for lunch when accompanied with a side salad.

Yield: 1 Tart

Ingredients:
1 sheet frozen puff pastry
2 tablespoons fresh parsley, chopped
1 tablespoon fresh rosemary, minced
1/4 teaspoon salt
1/4 teaspoon black pepper
1 cup plain Greek yogurt
1/2 cup finely chopped green onions, finely chopped
1 can artichoke hearts, quartered
½ cup goat cheese, crumbled
1/2 cup Parmesan cheese, shredded
2 eggs

Method of Preparation:
1. Preheat oven to 375 degrees.
2. Remove pastry from freezer and allow to sit at room temperature for at least 30 minutes.
3. In a large bowl, combine eggs, yogurt, onions, spices and parsley until fully blended.
4. Line a baking sheet with parchment paper, and unfold pastry onto sheet.
5. To avoid dough puffing up during baking, insert a fork throughout the dough as well as around the edges.

6. Pinch or fold up the edges of the dough to form a crust.
7. Layer artichokes on crust, then goat cheese, and finally the filling.
8. Sprinkle with parmesan cheese.
9. Bake for 30 minutes or until golden and filling is set.

SAUSAGE ROLL

The English variation of a standard hotdog, this recipe is most practical when feeding a large crowd. Consider serving with ketchup or cheese for an elegant take on classic snack food.

Yield: 24 Rolls

Ingredients:

1 sheet frozen puff pastry
1 1/2 pounds sausage
1 teaspoon basil, dried
1 teaspoon oregano, dried
1 teaspoon thyme, dried
2 eggs
Salt and pepper

Method of Preparation:
1. Preheat oven to 375 degrees
2. Remove pastry from freezer and allow to sit at room temperature for at least 30 minutes.
3. In a large bowl combine pork and spices, and blend with hands until mixed. Set aside.
4. Line a baking sheet with parchment paper and set aside.
5. Unfold pastry onto lightly floured countertop.
6. Roll seasoned sausage meat into a log, approximately one inch thick, long enough to match the length of the pastry.
7. Layer sausage log on top of pastry so they are equal length, and roll the pastry over the sausage, covering it complete so there is just a bit of overlap.
8. Repeat with remaining sausage and pastry, until all is used.
9. In a small bowl, beat egg and brush pastry with egg wash.
10. Using a lightly floured knife, cut pastry covered sausage into 2 inch rolls.
11. Transfer individual rolls to baking sheet.
12. Bake 15 minutes or until golden.

Zucchini Ricotta Tart

Nutrient dense, the zucchini and squash combine with ricotta cheese for a tart that is filling but not heavy. Perfect for summer or fall dinner, this tart is full of flavor and substance, and comes together in no time. Take a few extra minutes to play with the layer of the zucchini and squash if you prefer a tart with a festive design.

Yield: 1 Tart

Ingredients:
1 sheet frozen puff pastry
1 cup ricotta cheese
1 tablespoon honey
1 tablespoon fresh thyme
1 teaspoon water
1 tablespoon olive oil
1 zucchini
1 yellow summer squash
1 garlic clove
1/4 cup mozzarella cheese, shredded
1/2 cup Parmesan cheese, grated
1 egg white
1 egg yolk
¼ cup fresh basil, chopped

Method of Preparation:
1. Preheat oven to 400 degrees
2. Remove pastry from freezer and allow to sit at room temperature for at least 30 minutes.
3. Line a baking sheet with parchment paper and unfold pastry dough on top. Set aside.

4. Slice squash and zucchini into thin circles. Toss circles with a teaspoon of salt and lay them between two sheets of paper towels to dry.
5. In a medium bowl combine egg white, garlic, honey, ricotta cheese, thyme, mozzarella and Parmesan.
6. Spread cheese mix over dough, avoiding the inch or so closest to the edge.
7. Layer zucchini and squash slices over the cheese mix, again avoiding the outer edge of the dough.
8. Pinch or fold over the edges of the dough to create a raised crust.
9. In a small bowl mix water and egg yolk together, then brush over top of finished pastry.
10. Drizzle with olive oil and add salt and pepper to taste.
11. Bake 15 minutes or until golden.
12. Remove from oven and top with basil.

Pesto Tart

Rich and savory, the pesto blends with the ricotta and Parmesan cheese for a tart that is classic in taste, full of flavor, and easy to create. Ready in no time, this is a sophisticated dish that could be served for any meal. Feel free to make your own pesto to include, however your favorite store bought variation would be just as sufficient.

Yield: 1 Tart

Ingredients:
1 sheet frozen puff pastry
1 cup ricotta cheese
1 leek, sliced thin
2 eggs
2 egg whites
½ cup parmesan, grated
2 tablespoons butter
4 tablespoons heavy whipping cream
3 tablespoons pesto
2 tablespoons parsley, chopped
salt and pepper to taste

Method of Preparation:
1. Preheat oven to 375 degrees.
2. Remove pastry from freezer and allow to sit at room temperature for at least 30 minutes.
3. Over medium heat, melt butter in a medium frying pan.
4. Add sliced leeks and toss to coat, let cook until soft.
5. Combine egg, cream, ricotta, egg whites, pesto, parsley and parmesan in a medium bowl and stir to mix.
6. Line a baking sheet with parchment paper and unfold pastry dough on top.

7. Spread cheese mix over dough, avoiding the inch or so closest to the edge.
8. Top with leeks.
9. Pinch or fold up the edges of the dough to create a raised crust.
10. Bake 30 minutes or until golden.

Prosciutto and Pesto Puffs

A sandwich taken to the next level, substitute your bread slices for thin, flaky puff pastry. The result is a creative, elegant variation of a standard staple that takes very little time to prep or make.

Yield: 3 Puff Sandwiches

Ingredients:
1 sheet frozen puff pastry
6 slices prosciutto
¼ cup pesto

Method of Preparation
1. Preheat oven to 400 degrees.
2. Remove pastry from freezer and allow to sit at room temperature for at least 30 minutes.
3. On a well-floured surface, cut each sheet of dough into six equal size squares.
4. Line a baking sheet with parchment paper.
5. Move pastry squares to the parchment paper.
6. Bake for 12 minutes or until golden and puffed up.
7. Remove pastries from oven and transfer to wire rack to cool completely.
8. To serve, spread a layer of pesto and two prosciutto slices between two pastry squares.

Smoked Salmon Puffs

Always a party favorite, serve these elegant and refined appetizers at your next gathering. Salmon puffs give the illusion of significant time and effort yet this recipe is quick and easy, coming together in little time with minimal ingredients.

Yield: 36 Puffs

Ingredients:
1 sheet frozen puff pastry
2 cups smoked salmon, in bite sized pieces
1 ½ cups sour cream
1 cup fresh chives

Method Of Preparation:
1. Preheat oven to 400 degrees.
2. Remove pastry from freezer and allow to sit at room temperature for at least 30 minutes.
3. On a well-floured surface, cut each sheet of dough into thirty six, bite sized squares.
4. Line a baking sheet with parchment paper.
5. Move pastry squares to the parchment paper.
6. Bake for 12 minutes or until golden and puffed up.
7. Remove pastries from oven and transfer to wire rack to cool completely.
8. To serve, spread a layer of sour cream over a pastry square and top with a piece of salmon and dusting of chives.
9. Serve immediately.

PASTRY SLIDERS

An innovative twist to a classic dish, this hamburger remix is delightful and fun. When topped with cheese or your favorite condiments, be sure to serve immediately.

Yield: 6 Sliders

Ingredients:
2 sheets frozen puff pastry
½ pound ground turkey, beef, or other meat substitute.
1 teaspoon garlic, fresh and chopped
Salt and pepper
Lettuce, tomatoes, onions, avocado and other burger fixings.
Mayonnaise, ketchup, or condiment of your choice, to serve.

Method of Preparation
1. Preheat oven to 400 degrees.
2. Remove pastry from freezer and allow to sit at room temperature for at least 30 minutes.
3. On a well-floured surface, cut each sheet of dough into six squares.
4. Line a baking sheet with parchment paper.
5. Move pastry squares to the parchment paper.
6. Bake for 12 minutes or until golden and puffed up.
7. Remove pastries from oven and transfer to wire rack to cool completely.
8. While baking, prepare burgers with garlic and salt and pepper, and fry or grill to desired doneness.
9. To serve, layer burger between two puff pastry circles and dress with toppings and condiments of your choice.
10. Serve immediately.

Shrimp Wrapped Puff

A spin on a classic appetizer, this shrimp wrapped puff is a perfect dish to pass or serve, especially with a yield of 18 servings. Stuffed with creamy herb cheese and bacon, this dish is simple and unexpected.

Yield: 18 Puffs

Ingredients:
1 sheet frozen puff pastry
⅔ cup garlic herb cheese, soft and spreadable
18 jumbo shrimp, fresh peeled and butterflied with tail on
2 slices bacon, crumbled
1 tablespoon parsley, fresh and chopped

Method of Preparation:
1. Preheat oven to 400 degrees.
2. Remove pastry from freezer and allow to sit at room temperature for at least 30 minutes.
3. Line a baking sheet with parchment paper and set aside.
4. Combine cooked bacon crumbled, parsley and cheese into medium sized bowl, and stir until combined.
5. Fill center of each shrimp with a scoop of bacon cheese mix.
6. Unfold pastry dough on lightly floured surface.
7. Slice dough into 18 strips about ½ of an inch wide.
8. One a time, wrap each pastry strip around a single shrimp and place on baking sheet.
9. Continue with remaining shrimp until all are wrapped.
10. Bake for 12 minutes or until pastry is golden.

Curry and Beef Pie

An ideal entree for a chilly evening, this dish is comfort food taken to the next level. This savory dish is filled with complex flavors and spices yet remains delightfully simple to make.

Yield: 4 Pies

Ingredients:
4 sheets frozen puff pastry
1 pound ground beef
1 large russet potato
1 medium onion, chopped
¼ cup peas
1 tablespoon curry powder
1 tablespoon soy sauce
1 teaspoon vegetable oil
½ teaspoon sugar
1/4 teaspoon salt
1 egg
6 tablespoons water

Method of Preparations:
1. Combine beef, sugar, salt, and soy sauce in a medium bowl and mix well.
2. Over medium high heat, heat oil in a skillet before adding beef and cooking until browned.
3. Drain, reserving liquid, and set both meat aside.
4. Return liquid to skillet and reheat, adding onions and cooking those until translucent and soft.
5. Add potatoes and for several minutes until they begin to soften, then add curry powder, and stir until combined.

6. Add water to skillet and cook until potatoes are tender, and water is absorbed, approximately another minute.
7. Add peas and cooked beef to skillet, stir until combined, then remove from heat.
8. Allow to cool to room temperature, stirring occasionally.
9. Preheat oven to 375 degrees.
10. Remove pastry from freezer and allow to sit at room temperature for at least 30 minutes.
11. Line a baking sheet with parchment paper and set aside.
12. Unfold pastry dough on lightly floured surface.
13. Using a cup or a cookie cutter, cut 4 circles approximately five inches in diameter for a total of eight circles.
14. Spoon ⅓ of filling into four of the rounds, avoiding the outermost half of an inch around the edges.
15. Take another circle, and enclose filling covered circle, firmly sealing edges together.
16. Complete with remaining pies, and transfer to baking sheet.
17. Brush with egg wash.
18. Bake 30 minutes or until golden, allow to cool for five minutes before serving.

Puff Pastry "Caps"

Use this recipe as in conjunction with your favorite soup or pot pie recipe. When baked in ramekins, this will create very polished and elegant single servings. Yet when served deep mugs, your comfort food is taken to another level. Feel free to use a cookie cutter to create dough circles if you prefer that look instead.

Yield: 6 Caps

Ingredients:
1 sheet frozen puff pastry
8 cups of soup or pot pie mix, precooked and cooled
1 egg

Method of Preparation:
1. Preheat oven to 400 degrees.
2. Remove pastry from freezer and allow to sit at room temperature for at least 30 minutes.
3. On a well-floured surface, cut each sheet of dough into six equal size squares.
4. Fill six mugs or ramekins (or any desired serving dish) with equal portions of your soup or pot pie mix.
5. Place pastry squares on top of mix in each dish.
6. Bake for 12 minutes or until dough is golden and puffed up.

SWEET

Apple Tart

Classic and simple, the apple tart shines as a perennial favorite. Delicious any time of year, use your favorite baking apple to layer on top of the flaky pastry for a versatile dish appropriate for your most festive celebration or following any weeknight dinner.

Yield: 1 Tart

Ingredients:
1 sheet frozen puff pastry
⅓ cup sliced almonds
3 tablespoons brown sugar
2 tablespoons butter, unsalted and chilled
½ teaspoon almond extract
3 large apples

Method of Preparation:
1. Preheat oven to 375 degrees.
2. Remove pastry from freezer and allow to sit at room temperature for at least 30 minutes.
3. Line a baking sheet with parchment paper and unfold pastry dough on top.
4. Pinch or fold up the edges of the dough to create a raised crust.
5. Peel and slice apples into wedges about ⅛ inch thick.
6. Toss apples with sugar and almond extract in medium sized bowl.
7. Arrange apple slices on crust.
8. Chop butter into small cubes, and scatter over apple slices.
9. Sprinkle with almonds.
10. Bake 45 minutes or until golden.

Glazed Raspberry Strudel

A homemade variation of a childhood favorite, feel free to substitute the raspberry jam for any favorite flavor of preserve. For a particularly fancy touch, consider decorating the tops of these with sprinkles to really perfect the illusion.

Yield: 8 Strudels

Ingredients:
2 sheets frozen puff pastry
1 cup raspberry jam
1 cup confectioners sugar
¼ teaspoon vanilla extract
1 egg
2 teaspoons water

Method of Preparation:
1. Preheat oven to 375 degrees.
2. Remove pastry from freezer and allow to sit at room temperature for at least 30 minutes.
3. On a well-floured surface, cut each sheet of dough into eight equal size rectangles.
4. Line a baking sheet with parchment paper.
5. Move eight of the pastry rectangles to the parchment paper.
6. Scoop a heaping tablespoon of jam onto each rectangle, leaving about half an inch of dough exposed around each edge.
7. Repeat with seven remaining dough rectangles.
8. Separate egg white from yolk, and throw away whites.
9. Spread egg yolk over top of the eight rectangles that are not covered in jam.
10. Take egg covered rectangle, and place over jam covered rectangle, and use fingers to firmly seal pieces together.

11. Continue with remaining rectangles until all eight are stuffed and sealed..
12. Using a toothpick, poke holes throughout dough.
13. Bake for 35 minutes.
14. While baking combine sugar, vanilla and water together and beat until smooth.
15. Once finished baking, allow the pastries 15 minutes to cool before glazing.

APPLE APRICOT TART

While the apricot and apple blend together for a taste that is sure to please, and is more than sufficient when standing on its own, this tart begs to be served with a scoop of your favorite vanilla ice cream. This dish can be served warm or cold, so feel free to make ahead of time and store until serving.

Yield: 2 Tarts

Ingredients:

2 sheets frozen puff pastry
5 large apples
½ cup apricot preserves
4 tablespoons sugar
2 tablespoons butter
1 egg
2 teaspoons lemon juice

Method of Preparation:
1. Preheat oven to 400 degrees.
2. Remove pastry from freezer and allow to sit at room temperature for at least 30 minutes.
3. Line a baking sheet with parchment paper and unfold pastry dough on top.
4. Separate egg white from yolk, and throw away whites.
5. Spread egg yolk over the sides and top of dough.
6. Using a spoon or knife, smear pastry with the preserves.
7. Pinch or fold up the edges of the dough to create a raised crust.
8. Peel and slice apples into wedges about ⅛ inch thick.
9. Toss apples with sugar and juice of lemon in medium sized bowl.
10. Arrange apple slices on crust.
11. Chop butter into small cubes, and scatter over apple slices.
12. Bake 30 minutes or until golden.

Strawberry Napoleons

When finished, these Napoleons will look like miniature pastry sandwiches. Two pieces of pastry will surround a bed of whipped cream and strawberries. The amount of strawberries and cream you top with can be modified to your liking.

Yield: 3 Napoleons

Ingredients:
1 sheet frozen puff pastry
1 tub cool whip
½ cup cream cheese
1 cup fresh strawberries
1 cup milk
2 tablespoons milk
1 tablespoon powdered sugar
1 package instant pudding, vanilla flavored
¼ cup chocolate shavings

Method of Preparation:
1. Preheat oven to 400 degrees.
2. Remove pastry from freezer and allow to sit at room temperature for at least 30 minutes.
3. On a well-floured surface, cut each sheet of dough into six equal size squares.
4. Line a baking sheet with parchment paper.
5. Move pastry squares to the parchment paper.
6. Bake for 12 minutes or until golden and puffed up.
7. While baking, combine cool whip, milk, and pudding and beat until smooth and thick.
8. Allow mix to cool in fridge for 15 minutes or until firm.

9. Remove pastries from oven and transfer to wire rack to cool completely.
10. To serve, layer a serving of the mix between two pastry squares and top with strawberries.
11. Sprinkle with chocolate shavings and powdered sugar.

APPLE STRUDEL

This delicious, individual sized treat is perfect for a luxurious breakfast or a simple dessert. The apple mix is enclosed inside a pocket of buttery, flaky dough, and then baked until golden. When finished, these strudels will look complex, but are delightfully simple to make.

Yield: 8 Strudels

Ingredients:
2 Sheets frozen puff pastry
1 cup powdered sugar
½ cup brown sugar
3 tablespoons butter, unsalted and divided
1 tablespoon all-purpose flour
1 teaspoon vanilla
½ teaspoon cinnamon
½ cup cream cheese
2 large apples
1 egg
2 teaspoons lemon juice

Method of Preparation:
1. Using large holes of a box grater, grate apples.
2. Over medium heat, melt 2 tablespoons of butter in a saucepan.
3. When melted, add grated apple and toss until combined.
4. Mix in flour, lemon juice, brown sugar, cinnamon and salt.
5. Allow to cook, stirring often, until mix is syrupy and thick, approximately 8-10 minutes.
6. Remove from heat.
7. Take remaining tablespoon of butter and add into warm mix.
8. Allow to cool to room temperature.
9. Preheat oven to 375 degrees.

10. Remove pastry from freezer and allow to sit at room temperature for at least 30 minutes.
11. On a well-floured surface, cut each sheet of dough into eight equal size rectangles.
12. Line a baking sheet with parchment paper.
13. Move eight of the pastry rectangles to the parchment paper.
14. Scoop a heaping tablespoon of mix onto each rectangle, leaving about half an inch of dough exposed around each edge.
15. Repeat with seven remaining dough rectangles.
16. Separate egg white from yolk, and throw away whites.
17. Spread egg yolk over top of the eight rectangles that are not covered in apple mix.
18. Take egg covered rectangle, and place over apple mix rectangle, and use fingers to firmly seal pieces together.
19. Continue with remaining rectangles until all eight are stuffed and sealed.
20. Using a toothpick, poke holes throughout dough.
21. Bake for 35 minutes.
22. While baking, combine cream cheese, powdered sugar, and vanilla together and beat until smooth.
23. Once finished baking, allow the pastries 15 minutes to cool before frosting.

Rhubarb Galette

The perfect early spring dessert, consider this galette when the rhubarb crop is at its finest. When finished baking, the pastry is glazed with a delicious orange sauce, creating a very complex layering of flavors and textures.

Yield: 1 Galette

Ingredient:
1 sheet frozen puff pastry
½ cup sugar
1 cup orange juice
¾ pound rhubarb, stalks only, sliced thin
1 tablespoon lime juice
½ teaspoon orange, zested

Method of Preparation:
1. Preheat oven to 400 degrees.
2. Remove pastry from freezer and allow to sit at room temperature for at least 30 minutes.
3. In a bowl, combine orange juice, sugar, and lime juice.
4. Add rhubarb to mix, and let mix sit for ten minutes.
5. Line a baking sheet with parchment paper and unfold pastry dough on top, rounding dough into a circular shape.
6. Using knife or toothpick, poke holes all over pastry dough.
7. Pour rhubarb mix through a strainer set over a bowl, and keep liquid.
8. Layer rhubarb slices over dough, overlapping as necessary, but avoiding the outermost edge of the dough by one inch
9. Pinch or fold up the edges of the dough to create a raised crust, slightly layered over the rhubarb.
10. Bake for 30 minutes.

11. While baking, take remaining liquid and boil until reduced to ¼ cup.
12. Once baking is completed, transfer to wire rack and allow to cool before brushing with glaze and zest.

Strawberry Balsamic Tartlets

The use of reduction makes this simple tart incredibly sophisticated. If the combination seems unexpected, be prepared for surprise. The honey and balsamic add the perfect amount of balance to the sweet strawberries for a tart with exceptional depth of flavor.

Yield: 4 Tarts

Ingredients:
1 sheet frozen puff pastry
2 tablespoons sugar
½ cup white wine
⅛ cup balsamic vinegar
1 ½ tablespoons honey
2 cups strawberries, thinly sliced

Method of Preparation:
1. Preheat oven to 425 degrees.
2. Remove pastry from freezer and allow to sit at room temperature for at least 30 minutes.
3. On a well-floured surface, cut each sheet of dough into four equal size squares.
4. Line a baking sheet with parchment paper.
5. Move pastry squares to the parchment paper.
6. Pinch or fold up the edges of the dough to create a raised crust.
7. Using knife or toothpick, poke holes all over pastry dough.
8. Layer sliced strawberries on pastry dough, leaving a small amount of room around the edges.
9. Sprinkle each square with sugar.
10. Bake for 20 minutes or until golden.
11. While baking, combine balsamic, honey and wine in a sauce pan.

12. Bring to a boil and reduce heat.
13. Stir until mixture is about half the amount it started at.
14. Continue to cook until thick, and remove from heat.
15. Remove tarts from oven and allow to cool for five minutes before drizzling with reduction.

Nutella Pastry Puffs

When finished, these puffs will look like little sandwiches; two puffs surrounding a bed of rich Nutella mixture. The bananas add a perfect amount of soft texture to this flaky, creamy dish.

Yield: 9 Puffs

Ingredients:
2 sheets frozen puff pastry
¾ cup powdered sugar
¾ cup Nutella
1 tub cool whip
2 bananas, thinly sliced
Whipped cream, optional, for topping

Method of Preparation:
1. Preheat oven to 400 degrees.
2. Remove pastry from freezer and allow to sit at room temperature for at least 30 minutes.
3. On a well-floured surface, cut each sheet of dough into nine equal size squares.
4. Line a baking sheet with parchment paper.
5. Move pastry squares to the parchment paper.
6. Bake for 12 minutes or until golden and puffed up.
7. While baking, combine cool whip, powdered sugar, and Nutella and beat until smooth and thick.
8. Allow Nutella mix to cool in fridge for 15 minutes or until firm.
9. Remove pastries from oven and transfer to wire rack to cool completely.
10. To serve, layer a serving of the Nutella mix between two pastry squares and top with bananas and whipped cream.

Cinnamon Twists

The no-mess cinnamon roll alternative, these twists have the flavor and flakiness you would expect without the insanely sticky hands. To complete the experience, serve with a small bowl of frosting to dip the twists into.

Yield: 12 Twists

Ingredients:
1 sheet frozen puff pastry
2 tablespoons butter
3 tablespoons brown sugar
¾ teaspoon cinnamon
1 tablespoon milk
¼ teaspoon vanilla
1/2 cup cream cheese
1/4 cup icing sugar

Method of Preparation:
1. Preheat oven to 400 degrees.
2. Remove puff pastry from freezer and allow to sit at room temperature for thirty minutes.
3. Mix cinnamon and sugar together in small bowl and set aside.
4. Line a baking sheet with parchment paper and set aside.
5. On a lightly floured surface, roll pastry out flat.
6. Melt butter, and brush over rolled out pastry.
7. Toss cinnamon and sugar mix over buttered dough and lightly press mix into dough with a glass or rolling pin.
8. Cut 12 long, even strips out of dough using a knife or pizza cutter that has been lightly floured.
9. Using your hands, twist each piece and lay on baking sheet.
10. Bake for 10 minutes or until golden.

11. While baking, combine icing sugar, vanilla and cream cheese into medium bowl and beat until smooth.
12. Add milk and mix until combined, glaze should be thick but pourable.
13. Allow twists to cool before drizzling with glaze.

Nutella Roll Ups

Imagine the shape of a croissant when rolling these delicious little treats. For added flair, you can twist the sides of the pastry dough before baking for a truly authentic look. Rich and creamy, the shape will matter very little once you experience the combination of the flaky pastry and warm Nutella.

Yield: 12 Roll Ups

Ingredients:
2 sheets frozen puff pastry
1 cup Nutella
1 teaspoon water
1 egg

Method of Preparation:
1. Preheat oven to 400 degrees.
2. Remove pastry from freezer and allow to sit at room temperature for at least 30 minutes.
3. On a well-floured surface, cut each sheet of dough into six triangles for a total of twelve.
4. Line a baking sheet with parchment paper.
5. Move pastry squares to the parchment paper.
6. Take one small dollop of Nutella and place it at one tip of the triangle.
7. Roll dough so that Nutella is enclosed inside the crescent shaped dough.
8. Pinch edges of dough down to keep Nutella inside.
9. Repeat with 11 remaining triangles.
10. Mix water and egg together, and lightly brush egg wash over all stuffed crescents.
11. Bake for 20 minutes or until puffed up and golden.

Peach and Goat Cheese Turn Overs

There is something incredibly enticing about the combination of peach and goat cheese. The rich texture and depth of flavor are layered over the flaky pastry to create a divine treat.

Yield: 6 Turn Overs

Ingredients:
2 sheets frozen puff pastry
4 peaches, ripened and sliced into thin wedges
2 tablespoons of honey
½ cup goat cheese
1 teaspoon black pepper

Method of Preparation:

1. Preheat oven to 425 degrees.
2. Remove pastry from freezer and allow to sit at room temperature for at least 30 minutes.
3. On a well-floured surface, cut each sheet of dough into six equal size squares..
4. Line a baking sheet with parchment paper.
5. Move the pastry squares to the parchment paper.
6. Using knife or toothpick, poke holes all over pastry dough.
7. Angle each square so that they appear as a diamond shape, or two triangles with touching bases.
8. Evenly distribute goat cheese onto on half of the square, filling one of the "triangles" and spread evenly, stopping ½ inch away from the outer edge of the pastry.
9. Layer sliced peaches on cheese and pastry dough, leaving a small amount of room around the edges.

10. Sprinkle each square with pepper.
11. Fold the empty half of the square, the remaining "triangle" over on top of the square and using your fingers or a fork, carefully seal the turn over closed.
12. Finished pastry shape should resemble a triangle.
13. Bake for 20 minutes or until golden.
14. Remove tarts from oven and allow to cool for five minutes before drizzling with honey.

Triple Berry Tart

This recipe calls for strawberries, blackberries and raspberries, but feel free to substitute your favorite berry or whatever you have on hand. Either way, when preparing to serve, take a minute to create a beautiful design or pattern with your berries, as the contrast against the golden pastry and creamy base is marvellous.

Yield: 1 Tart

Ingredients:
1 sheet frozen puff pastry
¼ cup icing sugar
1 cup cream cheese
½ teaspoon vanilla
2 cups strawberries, sliced thin
1 cup raspberries
1 cup blackberries

Method of Preparation:
1. Preheat oven to 400 degrees.
2. Remove pastry from freezer and allow to sit at room temperature for at least 30 minutes.
3. Line a baking sheet with parchment paper and unfold pastry dough on top.
4. Pinch or fold up the edges of the dough to create a raised crust.
5. Using knife or toothpick, poke holes all over pastry dough.
6. Bake for 15 minutes or until golden, and then transfer to wire rack to cool completely.
7. Beat icing sugar, vanilla and cream cheese together until smooth.
8. Spread over cooled pastry and use spatula to smooth.
9. Cover cream cheese tart with berries.

PUFF CANDY BITES

You will need a mini muffin tin for this charming little treat. Perfect for a Halloween party, or any time you want to serve a mini version of your favorite candy. Consider this the perfect task for the littlest of bakers, as the simplicity of this recipe will stun you. Consider topping with a small amount of melted chocolate or sprinkles for additional flare.

Yield: 50 Bites

Ingredients:
2 Sheets frozen puff pastry
50 miniature / bite sized chocolate based candy bars

Method of Preparation:
1. Preheat oven to 400 degrees.
2. Remove pastry from freezer and allow to sit at room temperature for at least 30 minutes.
3. Fill mini muffin tin with mini muffin cups.
4. On a lightly floured surface, unroll dough and cut each sheet into 25 two inch squares for a total of 50.
5. Take one bite size candy bit and place it in the center of a dough square.
6. Fold the edges of the dough square around the candy bit, enclosing it completely.
7. Place the seam edge down in the muffin cup.
8. Repeat with remaining dough squares and candies.
9. Bake ten minutes or until golden.

Nutella Pastry

Golden, flaky pastry, rich and creamy Nutella come together in this recipe to create a treat that is simple and straightforward. The hazelnuts add additional texture and character, and are definitely recommended when putting this dish together.

Yield: 1 Pastry

Ingredients:
1 sheet frozen puff pastry
1 tablespoon sugar
1 cup Nutella
1 egg
4 tablespoons hazelnuts, chopped

Method of Preparation:
1. Preheat oven to 400 degrees.
2. Remove pastry from freezer and allow to sit at room temperature for at least 30 minutes.
3. Line a baking sheet with parchment paper and unfold pastry dough on top.
4. Pinch or fold up the edges of the dough to create a raised crust.
5. Using knife or toothpick, poke holes all over pastry dough.
6. Bake for 15 minutes or until golden, and then transfer to wire rack to cool completely.
7. Spread Nutella over cooled pastry and use spatula to smooth.
8. Sprinkle Nutella pastry with hazelnuts.

COCONUT PUMPKIN ROLL UPS

When finished, these little rolls should resemble the shape of croissants. While the combination of pumpkin and coconut may seem unexpected, it is truly a splendid mix, fresh and creamy tucked inside the flaky pastry. Sure to surprise and impress, this dish is simple to make.

Yield: 6 Roll Ups

Ingredients:

1 sheet frozen puff pastry
1 package instant pudding, vanilla flavored
3/4 cup canned pumpkin
1/2 cup coconut milk, unsweetened
3/4 teaspoon ground cinnamon
1 egg

Method of Preparation:
1. In a medium bowl, combine pudding mix, pumpkin, coconut milk and cinnamon.
2. Beat until smooth, and move to fridge to set.
3. Preheat oven to 400 degrees.
4. Remove pastry from freezer and allow to sit at room temperature for at least 30 minutes.
5. On a well-floured surface, cut sheet of dough into six triangles.
6. Line a baking sheet with parchment paper.
7. Move pastry squares to the parchment paper.
8. Take one small dollop of mix and place it at one tip of the triangle.
9. Roll dough so that mix is enclosed inside the crescent shaped dough.
10. Pinch edges of dough down to keep mix inside.
11. Repeat with remaining triangles.
12. Mix water and egg together, and lightly brush egg wash over all stuffed crescents.
13. Bake for 20 minutes or until golden.

Raspberry Lemon Napoleons

These Napoleons should resemble little sandwiches when finished. Berries and cream are layered in between two flaky pastry pieces for a beautiful finished product that is practically effortless to make.

Yield: 3 Napoleons

Ingredients:
1 sheet frozen puff pastry
1 cup fresh raspberries
⅔ cup powdered sugar
½ cup heavy cream
1 cup lemon curd

Method of Preparation:
1. Preheat oven to 400 degrees.
2. Remove pastry from freezer and allow to sit at room temperature for at least 30 minutes.
3. On a well-floured surface, cut each sheet of dough into six equal size squares.
4. Line a baking sheet with parchment paper.
5. Move pastry squares to the parchment paper.
6. Bake for 12 minutes or until golden and puffed up.
7. While baking, beat heavy cream until smooth and thick, then add sugar and mix again until forming peaks.
8. Remove pastries from oven and transfer to wire rack to cool completely.
9. To serve, layer a serving of the whipped cream and raspberries between two pastry squares..
10. Sprinkle with powdered sugar.

Cinnamon Puffs

You will need a mini muffin tin for these bite sized treats. Perfect for when you need individual servings, these are practically effortless to make and come together in no time.

Yield: 24 Puffs

Ingredients:
1 sheet frozen puff pastry
1 cup cream cheese
½ cup powdered sugar
1 teaspoon cinnamon

Method of Preparation:
1. Preheat oven to 400 degrees.
2. Remove pastry from freezer and allow to sit at room temperature for at least 30 minutes.
3. Fill mini muffin tin with mini muffin cups.
4. On a lightly floured surface, unroll dough and cut each sheet into 24 two inch squares.
5. In a medium sized bowl, beat cream cheese, powdered sugar and cinnamon until smooth and blended.
6. Place one spoonful of mix in the center of one puff square.
7. Fold the edges of the dough square around the mix, enclosing it completely.
8. Place the seam edge down in the muffin cup.
9. Repeat with remaining dough squares and mix.
10. Bake ten minutes or until golden.

Pear Ginger Tart

The spice of fresh ginger and the mild tang of ripe pears create a perfect balance of flavors in this flaky tart. To add a bit of sweetness, consider topping with a dollop of whipped cream or vanilla ice cream.

Yield: 1 Tart

Ingredients:
1 sheet frozen puff pastry
2 pears, sliced thin
1 tablespoon ginger, fresh and minced
1 tablespoon vanilla
2 tablespoons unsalted butter
1 tablespoon brown sugar
1 tablespoon sugar
1/2 tablespoon cinnamon

Method of Preparation:
1. Preheat oven to 400 degrees.
2. Remove pastry from freezer and allow to sit at room temperature for at least 30 minutes.
3. In a bowl, melt butter.
4. Combine with brown sugar, vanilla, ginger, and cinnamon. Set aside..
5. Line a baking sheet with parchment paper and unfold pastry dough on top.
6. Pinch or fold up the edges of the dough to create a raised crust.
7. Using knife or toothpick, poke holes all over pastry dough.
8. Brush half of the butter mix over dough.
9. Layer pear slices over dough, overlapping as necessary.
10. Brush with remaining butter mix and dust with sugar.
11. Bake for 15 minutes or until golden.

Peach Tart

A classic stone fruit, peach is delicious, and a favorite among many. Use a particularly ripe piece for this recipe for a sweet taste with a substantial amount of flavor. If interested in additional flavors or added complexity of taste, consider adding other stone fruits, such as nectarines, for a bold combination.

Yield: 1 Tart

Ingredients:
1 sheet frozen puff pastry
3 cups sliced peaches
1 teaspoon sugar
1 tablespoon lemon juice
1 egg, beaten
3 tablespoons honey

Method of Preparation:
1. Preheat oven to 375 degrees.
2. Remove pastry from freezer and allow to sit at room temperature for at least 30 minutes.
3. Combine peaches, lemon juice and honey. Set aside.
4. Line a baking sheet with parchment paper and unfold pastry dough on top.
5. Pinch or fold up the edges of the dough to create a raised crust.
6. Using knife or toothpick, poke holes all over pastry dough.
7. Layer fruit mix over dough, overlapping as necessary.
8. Brush with egg wash and dust with sugar.
9. Bake for 25 minutes or until golden.

BERRY CHEESECAKE

The cheesecake mix is the highlight of this dish, adding a creamy texture and rich flavor the tart. While the recipe calls for an assortment of berries, feel free to substitute or add your favorite singular berry or combination of toppings.

Yield: 1 Cheesecake

Ingredients:
1 sheet frozen puff pastry
½ cup sugar
2 tablespoons granulated sugar
8 ounces cream cheese
3 tablespoons heavy cream
1 tablespoon vanilla
¼ cup lemon zest
¼ cup lemon juice
2 tablespoons butter
10 strawberries, sliced
2 cups raspberries
Powdered sugar for dusting

Method of Preparation:
1. Preheat oven to 400 degrees.
2. Remove pastry from freezer and allow to sit at room temperature for at least 30 minutes.
3. Line a baking sheet with parchment paper and unfold pastry dough on top.
4. Pinch or fold up the edges of the dough to create a raised crust.
5. Using knife or toothpick, poke holes all over pastry dough.
6. Bake for 15 minutes or until golden, and then transfer to wire rack to cool completely.

7. Beat cheesecake ingredients together until smooth.
8. Allow to sit in refrigerator until chilled, approximately 30 minutes.
9. Spread over cooled pastry and use spatula to smooth.
10. Cover cream cheese tart with berries.
11. Sprinkle with powdered sugar prior to serving.

APPLE CARAMEL TARTLETS

This classic apple tart is taken to a new level with the addition of the caramel sauce. Feel free to use your favorite store bought caramel sauce or to whip up a batch of your own, but consider the salted variation for an elevated level of taste dimension.

Yield: 6 Tartlets

Ingredients:
2 sheets frozen puff pastry
3 apples, sliced
½ teaspoon cinnamon
3 tablespoons granulated sugar
Salted caramel sauce

Method of Preparation:
1. Preheat oven to 400 degrees.
2. Remove pastry from freezer and allow to sit at room temperature for at least 30 minutes.
3. In a bowl combine sugar and cinnamon. Set aside.
4. Line a baking sheet with parchment paper and unfold pastry dough on top.
5. Pinch or fold up the edges of the dough to create a raised crust.
6. Using knife or toothpick, poke holes all over pastry dough.
7. Layer apple slices over dough, overlapping as necessary.
8. Dust with cinnamon sugar mix.
9. Bake for 15 minutes or until golden.
10. Let rest until fully cooled then drizzle with caramel sauce.

Raspberry and Brie Hand Pies

The savory taste of brie and the sweet raspberries come together to make a delicious treat. However, the use of dark chocolate and the drizzle of chocolate sauce make this simple treat incredibly delicious. Serve when cooled for an impressive, sophisticated snack.

Yields: 6 Hand Pies

Ingredients:
1 sheet frozen puff pastry
1 egg
1 cup raspberries
5 ounces brie, rind removed
½ cup dark chocolate, chopped
¼ cup chocolate sauce

Method of Preparation:
1. Preheat oven to 375 degrees.
2. Remove pastry from freezer and allow to sit at room temperature for at least 30 minutes.
3. Line a baking sheet with parchment paper and set aside.
4. To make these bites, the sheet of pastry will need to be cut into 12 rectangles to make 6 rectangle pockets.
5. Crack egg into small bowl and beat until smooth. Combine with tablespoon of milk.
6. Brush the egg wash over 12 of the rectangles.
7. Slice brie into small wedges and set on brushed rectangle.
8. Add several raspberries and some of the chopped chocolate on top of brie.
9. Layer the second pastry rectangle over the cheese and berries.
10. Using a fork and your fingers, tightly fold the edges together making sure to seal pastry closed.

11. Using a toothpick, poke a small hole into the center of the pastry.
12. Bake for 15 minutes or until crust is golden.
13. Allow to cool completely before drizzling with chocolate sauce.

Meyer Lemon Tart

When finished, the look of this tart is striking. Lemon circles cover the surface of the pastry for a bright and vibrant visual. When serving, make sure it is known that these circles will be delicious to eat, as the lemons used in this recipe are Meyer lemons, which are sweeter and have a thinner peel then a standard lemon.

Yield: 1 Tart

Ingredients:
1 sheet frozen puff pastry
6 Meyer lemons, sliced thin
1 cup heavy cream
1/2 vanilla bean
1 cup sugar
2 cups water
1 large egg

Method of Preparation:
1. In a saucepan over medium heat, combine water and granulated sugar and cook, stirring consistently, until sugar has dissolved.
2. Add sliced lemons to water, and simmer until lemons are soft and clear, approximately an hour and a half.
3. The lemon water will turn syrupy during this time. When the lemons are completed, remove them and transfer to a wire rack to drain.
4. Preheat oven to 400 degrees.
5. Remove pastry from freezer and allow to sit at room temperature for at least 30 minutes.
6. Line a baking sheet with parchment paper and unfold pastry dough on top.
7. Pinch or fold up the edges of the dough to create a raised crust.

8. Using knife or toothpick, poke holes all over pastry dough.
9. Dust with egg wash and sprinkle with sugar.
10. Return dough to freezer for thirty minutes or until firm.
11. Bake pastry for 20 minutes or until golden.
12. Allow to cool completely.
13. While baking, beat heavy cream and vanilla seeds together until forming peaks.
14. Layer lemon slices over dough, overlapping as necessary.
15. Serve topped with the vanilla cream.

BITE SIZED STRAWBERRY PASTRIES

These little pastries are the perfect balanced treat. They are sweet, but not overly so. The cream cheese and honey complete the strawberry flavor, and the overall result is a guilt free, flaky treat that quick and simple to create.

Yield: 20 Bites

Ingredients:
1 sheet frozen puff pastry
2 cups strawberries, sliced
3/4 cup cream cheese
2 tablespoons honey
1 egg

Method of Preparation:
1. Preheat oven to 400 degrees.
2. Remove pastry from freezer and allow to sit at room temperature for at least 30 minutes.
3. Line a baking sheet with parchment paper and set aside.
4. Unfold pastry dough on top lightly floured surface.
5. Use a cookie cutter to slice the pastry into small squares.
6. Transfer squares to parchment covered baking sheet.
7. Dust tops of pastry with egg wash.
8. Bake for 12 minutes or until golden.
9. Allow squares to cool
10. Once cooled, take a small dollop of cream cheese and spread over each square.
11. Top with strawberries and honey.

WHITE CHOCOLATE RASPBERRY TART

Creamy white chocolate and tart raspberries are layered on top of rich cream and flaky pastry. This luxurious combination is delicious and simple, taking just a few minutes to prepare and bake before being read to serve.

Yields: 1 Tart

Ingredients:
1 sheet frozen puff pastry
1 cup raspberries
1 egg,
½ cup cream cheese
1 cup heavy cream
4 tablespoons sugar
1 teaspoon vanilla
A pinch of salt
¼ cup white chocolate shavings

Method of Preparation:
1. Preheat oven to 400 degrees.
2. Remove pastry from freezer and allow to sit at room temperature for at least 30 minutes.
3. Line a baking sheet with parchment paper and unfold pastry dough on top.
4. Pinch or fold up the edges of the dough to create a raised crust.
5. Using knife or toothpick, poke holes all over pastry dough.
6. Brush with egg wash.
7. Bake pastry for 20 minutes or until golden.
8. Allow to cool completely.
9. While baking, beat cream cheese, vanilla, sugar and salt together until smooth.
10. Add heavy cream slowly while beating, and continue until peaks form. .
11. Pour cream into cooled pastry, and smooth with a spatula.
12. Layer raspberries and sprinkle with white chocolate shavings.

Chocolate Banoffee Pie

These small individual sized treats are stuffed with warm banana and melted chocolate. The result is gooey and warm dessert that is best served while still warm. Consider drizzling extra chocolate over the top of the slightly cooled pastry to add a touch of decadence.

Yields: 4 Pies

Ingredients:
1 sheet frozen puff pastry
2 bananas, sliced
16 squares of chocolate, chopped
4 tablespoons fudge sauce

Method of Preparation:
1. Preheat oven to 400 degrees.
2. Remove pastry from freezer and allow to sit at room temperature for at least 30 minutes.
3. Line a baking sheet with parchment paper set aside.
4. On a lightly floured surface, unroll dough and cut each sheet into 4 squares.
5. Take one bit of banana, a spoonful of sauce, and some chocolate pieces, and place in the center of a dough square.
6. Fold the edges of the dough square around the banana and chocolate, enclosing it completely.
7. Place the seam edge down on the baking sheet.
8. Repeat with remaining dough squares.
9. Bake ten minutes or until golden.

Printed in Great Britain
by Amazon